St. Thomas

United States Virgin Islands

St. Thomas

United States Virgin Islands

by Gerald Singer

Featuring the Photography of Don .Hebert

Sombrero Publishing Co., St. John, USVI

St. Thomas, United States Virgin Islands
by Gerald Singer

Photography by Don Hebert
Edited by Habiba Hussein
Design by Chelsea O'Brien

Printed in China by Everbest Printing Company Ltd.
Through Four Colour Imports, Ltd. Lousiville, Kentucky

LCCN 2007902611
ISBN 0-9790269-0-3

GOVERNOR JOHN P. deJONGH, JR

Governor John P. deJongh, Jr. and family at Government House,
overlooking the Charlotte Amalie Harbor. DeJongh was inaugurated
as the seventh elected Governor of the United States Virgin Islands
on January 1, 2007.

West End

Nearby Islands & Cays

CHARLOTTE AMALIE

& VICINITY

The Gateway to the Caribbean

'The place that is on the way to every other place,' is the mariners terse way of describing St. Thomas. When he lays his course for any part of the Caribbean Sea, the tip of his horny finger points to St. Thomas. To call the little island the gateway to the Caribbean is not mere poetic fancy. The shortened and best course from England to any Central American port, for steam or sail, is by St. Thomas. The route from Spain to Cuba or Mexico is by St. Thomas. For the lines from the United States to Brazil, the most convenient port of call is St. Thomas. To go from the Greater to the Lesser Antilles one goes by the way of St. Thomas…

- William Drysdale, *Harpers Weekly*,
January 20, 1900, "The Gateway to the Caribbean"

CHARLOTTE AMALIE

Charlotte Amalie is the capital and largest city of the U.S. Virgin Islands, with an estimated population of nearly 20,000.

Charlotte Amalie, also pronounced, Charlotte Amalia, was named after the queen consort of King Christian V of Denmark, Charlotte Amelia of Hesse-Cassel (1650-1714).

We can trace the town back to its humble beginnings in 1672, when four settlers were granted innkeeper licenses and permission to build their homes on the west side of Fort Christian.

Although the first European colonists arrived with the prospect of making their fortune in agriculture, it soon became evident that St. Thomas, with its excellent harbor, convenient geographical position and political status as a freeport, offered faster and greater financial rewards to merchants, traders and those involved with the servicing and maintenance of ships.

Such was the popularity and freewheeling nature of the town in its early days that the first unofficial name given to the city was *Taphaus*, meaning "pub" or "beer hall."

Describing the Charlotte Amalie Harbor in 1701, Dominican missionary Père Labat, known as "the pirate priest," wrote:

Denmark, being almost neutral in the wars of Europe, the port of St. Thomas is open to all nations. During peace it serves as an entrepôt for the commerce, which the French, English, Spaniards and Dutch do not dare to pursue openly on their own islands; and in time of war it is the refuge of merchant ships when pursued by privateers. On the other hand, the privateers send their prizes here to be sold when they are not disposed to send them to a greater distance. Many small vessels also proceed from St. Thomas to the coast of South America, whence they bring back much riches in specie, or in bars and valuable merchandise, In a word, St. Thomas is a market of consequence.

The Waterfront

As the importance of St. Thomas and its maritime economy grew, so did the town. Harbor frontage became very expensive. As a result, building lots tended to be long and narrow with just enough exposure to the harbor for the implementation of piers and boat slips.

For the same reason, wide streets were not employed to connect the waterfront to Main Street. Instead there were a series of narrow alleyways, still evident to this day. Private residences were built on the less expensive, landward side of the street and eventually on the valleys and hillsides adjacent to the harbor.

The 20th century brought automobiles to the island. Soon traffic on the steep, narrow streets of Charlotte Amalie became congested. In the 1940s, a project was commenced to fill in the harbor on the waterfront side of the commercial warehouses in order to construct what is now Veterans Highway, which runs along the harbor.

Charlotte Amalie has maintained much of its old character as both a bustling Caribbean seaport, hosting cruise ships, pleasure yachts and cargo vessels from all around the world, and as a shopping mecca, offering millions of visitors a treasure trove of duty-free shopping delights.

MAIN STREET

Dronningens Gade, now commonly known as
Main Street, dates back to the 17th century
and was the first street to be built after the
Danish colonization of the island.

STEP STREETS

A unique feature of Charlotte Amalie are "step streets." They were constructed so people living in the residential neighborhoods on the steep hillsides could have a more convenient access to town. The most familiar of these streets is Store Taarne Gade, better known as the "99 Steps," which run between the town and the top of Government Hill. "Ninety-nine Steps" is actually a misnomer. Those who care to count will find that there are, in fact, 103 steps.

Yacht Haven Grande

In the 1960s, 70s and 80s, St. Thomas was a charter yachting hub centering on the old Yacht Haven Marina. Salty charter boat captains could always be found at Fearless Freddy's Bar, exchanging tales of Virgin Island adventures at sea and awaiting potential charterers interested in anything from day sails to extended cruises to the British Virgin Islands and beyond.

The St. Thomas charter industry began a decline starting with the advent of "bareboat" charters, in which people would rent fully outfitted sail and motor vessels, a development, which in many ways better suited Tortola and the British Virgins.

In 1995, Hurricane Marilyn devastated the marina and the property was left to deteriorate.

It now appears that St. Thomas will enter a new era of yachting with the opening of the Yacht Haven Grande on March 18, 2007 in the location of the old Yacht Haven Hotel and Marina.

The modern Yacht Haven Grande will cater to the burgeoning megayacht industry featuring a state-of-the-art marina capable of handling 50 megayachts, including one slip, which would berth vessels up to 400 feet in length.

Additionally the complex houses restaurants, boutiques and condominiums.

When fully completed Yacht Haven Grande is slated to include a 70-room hotel, more retail businesses and restaurants, a private yacht club, office space, a water theme park, a public access dinghy dock and a conference center.

Fort Christian

The first expedition to St. Thomas in 1666 ended in failure; partly as a result of attacks by bands of privateers who helped themselves to the colonists' supplies, equipment and ships.

Understandably, the construction of a fort for the defense of the colony was a high priority for those who arrived on second expedition, led by Jørgen Iversen in May of 1672. Work began on the fort in 1673, which was named Fort Christian or Christiansfort, after Danish King Christian V. The site chosen was a prominent peninsula in the center of the harbor, which has since been filled.

Also in 1673, the first Africans were brought to St. Thomas as enslaved workers, one of whom was Simon Lamare, a talented mason. Lamare was acquired by Governor Iversen and offered a contract to oversee the construction of the fort for which he would be granted his freedom after seven years service. After fulfilling his obligations, Lamare became one of the first members of St. Thomas' important and influential free black society.

By 1676, the outer walls were completed, as well as a three-story oval tower containing cannon emplacements on the second and third floor and on the roof. Utilizing the strategic advantage of this walled fortification, soldiers at Fort Christian were able to repel an attack by French settlers from St. Croix in 1678.

The fort was demilitarized and renovated during the 1870s after which it served as the police headquarters and a jail. In 1983, Fort Christian became a museum exhibiting the history of the Virgin Islands, a collection of vintage furniture from the Danish period and an art gallery.

Fort Christian, now designated a National Historical Landmark, is located between Veterans Highway and Emancipation Garden in Charlotte Amalie. It is the oldest structure in the Virgin Islands. Major restoration and renovation of Fort Christian began in 1990 and is expected to be completed in 2007.

Frederik's Fort & Skytsborg

Fort Christian suffered from strategic vulnerability because an invading army could capture the hills above town and use that vantage point to set up cannons and bombard the fort from above. To prevent such an occurrence, the colonists constructed two fortified towers on the hills above the fort, Skytsborg Tower (Sky Tower) and Frederik's Fort. The two forts were originally constructed during the 1680s.

Skytsborg (photo on right) was later renamed Blackbeard's Tower, after the infamous pirate Edward Teach, a.k.a. Blackbeard. The tower is now part of "The Inn at Blackbeard's Castle."

Frederik's Fort (photo on facing page) was renamed Bluebeard's Castle after a legendary, but fictitious, pirate.

LEGISLATURE BUILDING

The Virgin Islands Legislature Building, originally built in 1828. It was destroyed by a devastating hurricane in 1867 and rebuilt in the 1870s. The structure has served as a military and police barracks, a health facility and as the St. Thomas High School. In 1917, it was the site of the official Transfer Ceremony whereby the United States took control of the islands from Denmark. The building assumed its present function as the headquarters for the Virgin Islands Legislature in 1957.

Haagensen House

Constructed in 1827, the Haagensen House, located at the top of the 99 steps, served as the home of Hans Haagensen and his wife Sarah Julia Magens. Now operated as a museum, the Haagensen House exhibits West Indian antiques from early 19th century, a time of unparalleled prosperity for the Danish colony.

VILLA BRITANNIA

Antique West Indian kitchen on display at Villa Britannia

VILLA NOTMAN

Villa Notman was originally constructed by Scottish engineer, Robert Notman in 1860 and served as his private residence. The construction is principally native stone and the yellow bricks, which served as ballast on the ships carrying enslaved Africans.

The cast iron double balcony was imported from New Orleans.

The top floor of the villa is now a museum, with exhibits of antique furniture from the West Indies, Europe and mainland America.

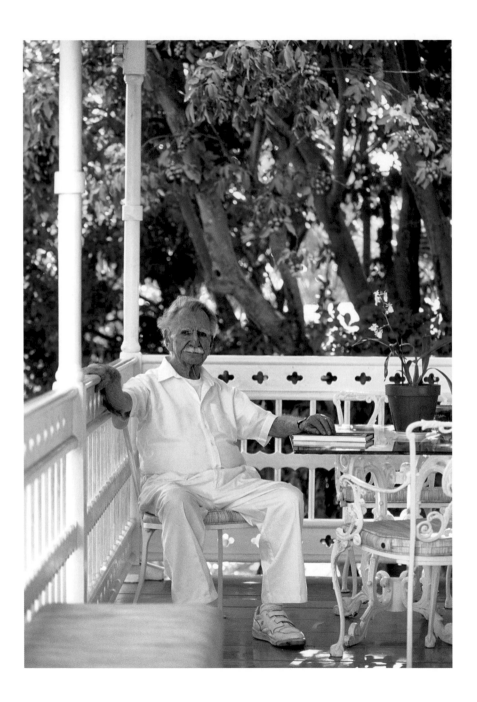

ISIDOR PAIEWONSKY

Isidor Paiewonsky was born on St. Thomas in 1909, when the Virgin Islands were still under Danish rule.

As a conservationist and philanthropist, Isidor Paiewonsky was greatly responsible for the donation of Paiewonsky family land on much of Hassel Island to the National Park. He is also said to be responsible for saving the environmentally crucial Mangrove Lagoon on the east end of St. Thomas. When the powers that be, including his brother, the Governor of the Virgin Islands, had slated the lagoon to be used for a jetport capable of handling large aircraft, Isidor spoke out in defense of the lagoon. As a more environmentally friendly alternative, the Cyril E. King Airport was expanded to meet the demands of most modern day jets.

As a St. Thomas businessman, Isidor Paiewonsky was instrumental in creating the duty-free retail industry, which today brings millions of tourist dollars to the territory.

As an author and historian, Paiewonsky is said to be the foremost chronicler of Virgin Islands history and has written several books on the subject.

Isidor Paiewonsky died at the age of 95 on December 6, 2004 on the island where he was born.

Sitting room at the residence of the late Isidor Paiewonsky

Religious Tolerance

Christianity arrived on St. Thomas with the first European settlers in 1666. The Lutheran Pastor, Kjeld Jensen Slagelse, who had run afoul of church authorities in Denmark, ministered to a congregation of some 100 parishioners, only half of whom were Danish Lutherans. The pastor also served as governor of the settlement when the original governor died.

This first expedition ended in failure due to high mortality from disease, hunger and raids by buccaneers and Pastor Slagelse sailed back to Denmark along with the few survivors of that ill-fated mission.

Pastor, Slagelse joined the next expedition to St. Thomas in 1671, but died aboard ship before reaching the island. He was succeeded by another minister, who died shortly after taking over the position. The third minister had to be sent back to Denmark for drunkenness. (The matter was turned over to the Danish courts where the minister argued that his drunken states were the result of the poor quality of rum: a white, unrefined, high alcohol content concoction known a "kill devil," produced on the island.)

Life expectancy of Lutheran ministers, as well as for many of the other colonists, was quite short. During the first 100 years that the Lutheran Church conducted services on St. Thomas, there were 31 different ministers.

Lutheran services were originally held in the courtyard of the fort and all colonists were required to attend services regardless of religious affiliation.

When settlers sent back accounts of hardship and disease, the Danes, who were generally comfortable at home, became extremely reluctant to settle the new territories. Even prisoners promised freedom after six years of labor on St. Thomas responded to the offer with riots and mutinies. In order to recruit settlers, the Danish government and its representative in the colonies, the Danish West India Company, resorted to inviting foreigners to settle the islands. One of the incentives employed to entice foreigners to settle on St. Thomas was the prospect of religious tolerance.

The majority of these foreign settlers on St. Thomas were Dutch. So influential were these foreigners that a Dutch Creole, called Creolsk soon became the common language of St. Thomas and St. John.

Cooperation and religious tolerance began with the Dutch being allowed to use the Lutheran Church inside the fort to conduct services until they were able to build a church of their own.

By 1675, the Dutch and French Reformed Churches had built churches just to the east of the fort. In 1685, Jews and Catholics were granted freedom of religion. In the early 1700s, an Anglican Church was set up to serve English settlers and in 1736, the Moravians established a slave mission on the island.

SYNAGOGUE

Jews were among the first settlers to St. Thomas and were granted religious freedom in 1685.

The small St. Thomas Jewish community founded their first synagogue in 1796.

By 1823, the Jewish community had grown large enough to necessitate the building of a larger synagogue. (The Jewish population peaked on St. Thomas at about 400 in the middle of the 19th century, making up about half of the island's white community.)

Beracha Veshalom Vegemilith or Blessing, Peace and Loving Deeds was built in 1833 and is the third oldest synagogue in the western hemisphere.

LUTHERAN CHURCH

The Lutheran Church on St. Thomas is the second oldest Lutheran Church in the western hemisphere. As the official church of Denmark, Lutheran ministers arrived with the first settlers and the first services were held in the courtyard of the fort.

In 1754, a church was built outside the fort and began ministering to blacks for the first time. Lutheran Ministers translated the Bible to Creole, and the same minister held services for two separate congregations, one Danish and the other Negro Creole.

The church was destroyed by a hurricane in 1772 and was replaced in 1789 by the Frederik Lutheran Church. The construction was financed by a free black parishioner, Jean Reeneaus.

The original Georgian-style building was reconstructed in 1827 after being destroyed by fire and then again in 1870, after damage suffered in a hurricane.

CRUISE SHIPS

Approximately 1,500,000 cruise ship passengers arrive on St. Thomas annually,
making St. Thomas the busiest cruise ship harbor in the West Indies.

Seaplane Service

The photo on the facing page shows a Seaborne Airlines deHavilland Twin Otter DHC-6 as it takes off from Charlotte Amalie Harbor on St. Thomas bound for Christainsted St. Croix.

Seaborne was not the first commercial seaplane service to operate in the Virgin Islands. That distinction belongs to Antilles Air Boats, started by flying ace, renowned test pilot and author Charlie Blair in 1964.

Charlie Blair distinguished himself, among countless other achievements, by flying his scarlet-red P-51 Mustang, named Excalibur III, non-stop from New York to London in 1951. In May of that same year Charlie Blair made the first solo flight over the North Pole delivering personally through the cockpit window a letter addressed to Santa Claus from his son, Chris. Excalibur III is now on permanent display at the National Air and Space Museum in Washington, D.C.

In 1968, Charlie Blair married the famous movie actress Maureen O'Hara and the couple lived on St. Croix.

By 1977, Antilles Air Boats, with a fleet of 23 amphibious aircraft including 19 Grumman Goose seaplanes, was making more than 100 flights a day, carrying some 250,000 passengers a year. Virgin Islanders often referred to Antilles Airboats as "The Streetcar Line of the Virgin Islands."

Charlie Blair died in 1978 when the Grumman Goose he was piloting developed engine trouble and crashed between St. Croix and St. Thomas.

EVERYBODY LOVE DE CARNIVAL

Everybody love de Carnival,
No don't stop de Carnival,
Do as you like, but leave my Carnival,
All West Indians love their Carnival,
Everybody bound to have their fun,
No rain at all can stop de Carnival,
Not even hurricanes can stop de Carnival,
because all de Creole dey love their Carnival.

- *Don't Stop the Carnival* by Duke of Iron
(Calypso theme song for Carnival 1952)

CARNIVAL

Adolph "Ding" Sixto was said to be the driving force behind St. Thomas' first carnival in 1912 by convincing the Main Street merchants to sponsor the affair which he would be economically, culturally and socially beneficial.

The Carnival King arrived at King's Wharf on a boat and then was carried to Rothschild Francis Square (Market Square) in a horse-drawn carriage for the coronation of the Carnival Queen. A parade marched from there to Emancipation Garden, where games, such as climbing the greased pole, the bag race and catching the greased pig, were played by both youngsters and adults.

A second carnival was held in 1914, with the celebrations lasting two days.

The advent of World War I, with its devastating effect on the shipping economy of St. Thomas, halted what was becoming an annual tradition until 1952, when carnival was formally revived. Since then, the carnival has been celebrated on an annual basis taking place during the last two weeks of April. The St. Thomas Carnival is now the second largest carnival in the Caribbean, topped only by the island of Trinidad.

Carnival features include music by popular calypso, scratch and steel drum bands, Moko Jumbies, a Children's Carnival with games and amusement park rides, and local foods.

Moko Jumbies

FOOD FAIR

Carnival Food Fair features such local delicacies as fried
fish, conch or whelk stews, lobster, johnny cakes, pates,
kalaloo, bull foot soup, goat water, maubi and sea moss.

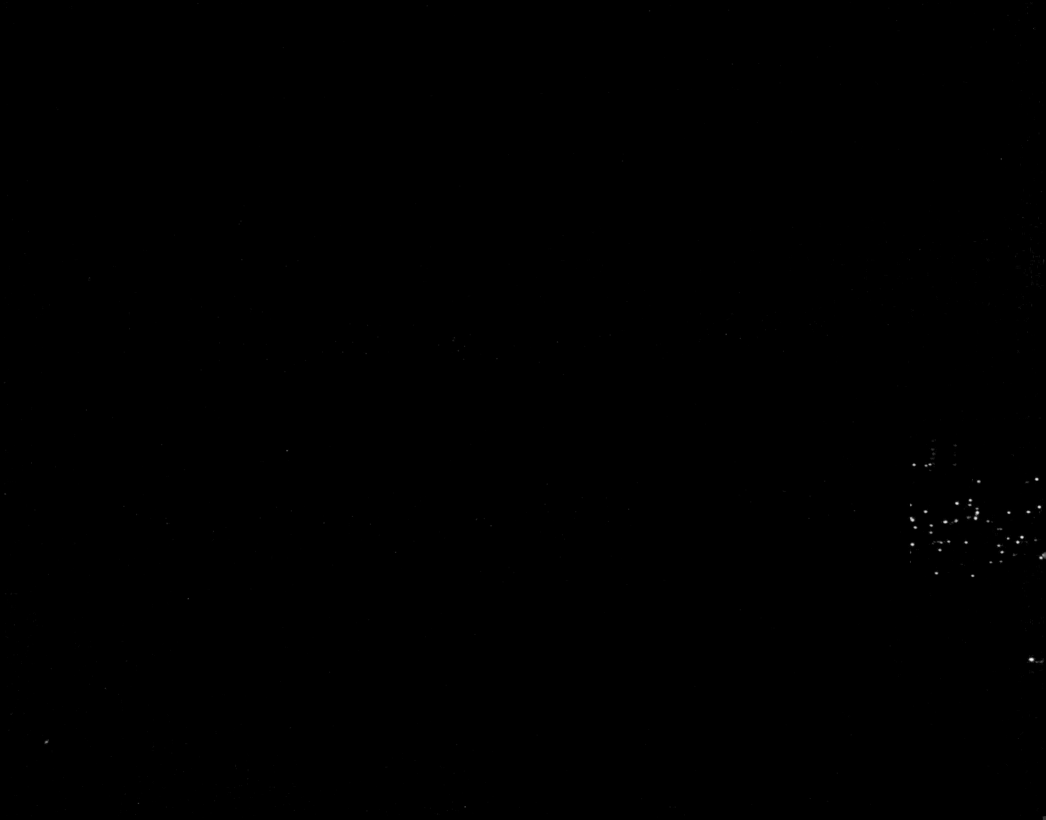

Frenchtown

During the 17th and 18th century, religious intolerance in France led to a horrible epoch of persecution for French Protestants, know as Huguenots. Their churches, homes, bibles and hymn books were burned and their children were taken away to be brought up by Catholic nuns. Thousands were burned at the stake, tortured, sent to sea to serve as galley slaves or condemned to prisons where chances of survival were slim.

An estimated 250,000 Huguenots lost their lives, while another 250,000 were able to leave France and settle elsewhere. One of these havens was the French West Indian Island of St. Bartholomew, better known as St. Barts.

A rocky and infertile landscape and lack of other economic opportunities led many of the descendants of the original refugees to emigrate to St. Thomas where they established two diverse communities, one alongside the harbor just south of downtown Charlotte Amalie that became known as Frenchtown and the other on the hills and valleys on the north side of the island.

The people of Frenchtown often turned to the sea for sustenance. The small village is famous for its fishing industry as well as for its fine restaurants. The Northside community, centered in Dorothea, Mandahl and Hull Bay, combines fishing with agriculture as a way of life.

SHOPPING

The old St. Thomas waterfront warehouse
district, located between Main Street and
Veterans Highway, is now the premier duty-
free shopping district of the Caribbean.

Shoppers can find great buys on jewelry,
gold, gemstones, wines and liquors,
perfumes, china, crystal, art, clothing,
electronics and more.

Other tourist-oriented shopping areas
include the cruise ship port at Havensight
Mall, Yacht Haven Grande, Crown Bay just
to the west of downtown and the American
Yacht Harbor in Red Hook.

ATLANTIS SUBMARINE

Submarine tourism was the brainchild of Dennis Hurd, who began his career at sea as captain of a 20-ton schooner sailing between Nova Scotia and the Bahamas

As a design engineer for International Hydrodynamics, a company that manufactured small manned submarines used for the inspection maintenance and repair of North Sea oil rigs Hurd would often bring along clients and company executives to inspect drilling sites, taking them down in compact submersibles to more than one mile below the surface of the sea. Observing the excitement and enthusiasm of his passengers, Hurd came upon the notion of underwater tourism and designed a submarine that would fulfill that purpose.

In 1985, Atlantis I, a 28-passenger submarine became the world's first tourist submarine operating out of the Cayman Islands and in 1987, Atlantis III, a 48-passenger sub, was launched on St. Thomas.

St. Thomas passengers are transported by motor launch from downtown Charlotte Amalie to the Atlantis dive site where they board the submarine for a 50-minute underwater adventure.

The adventure begins with a 20-foot dive and a passage alongside a vibrant coral reef. Descending to 80 feet, the Atlantis then navigates through an underwater canyon teeming with sea life. After a gradual ascent, the passengers board the launch for the scenic 20-minute cruise back to shore.

PARADISE POINT

Paradise Point is located near the summit of Flag Hill, overlooking Charlotte Amalie Harbor some 700 feet above the Caribbean Sea. Although accessible by road, the more adventurous can reach Paradise Point via a dramatic seven-minute cable car ride.

Having arrived, visitors can enjoy spectacular views from the extensive viewing deck offering a bird's eye view of town, the harbor and beyond all the way to St. Croix, Culebra, Vieques and the El Yunque Rainforest on Puerto Rico.

In addition to the magnificent view, Paradise Point offers a bar and restaurant, shopping, a nature trail and a tropical bird show.

Spectacular sunsets at Paradise Point are often accompanied by the music of local bands. Enjoy!

RESTAURANTS

The multiethnic, multicultural and multinational character of St. Thomas throughout its history is evident in the vast array of restaurants and cuisine available on the island. Caribbean, French, Middle Eastern and East Indian influences are joined by more recent dining trends such as Japanese, Chinese, Italian, and fast food. Restaurants range from small, informal Rastafarian "I-Tal" stands to elegant, pricey dining establishments. Most, but certainly not all of the restaurants are concentrated in the Downtown, East End and Frenchtown neighborhoods.

FRENCHMAN'S REEF & MORNINGSTAR BEACH

It's an easy hop to a world class Virgin Islands beach from bustling downtown Charlotte Amalie. Of course you can take a taxi or drive, but traveling by water is also an option via a 15-minute cruise on the motor launch, *Reefer*, a ferry that sails hourly between the Charlotte Amalie waterfront and the Mariott Frenchman's Reef Hotel dock.

The hotel is situated on a promontory at the head of the harbor enjoying spectacular views and refreshing sea breezes. Visitors can take advantage of several hotel facilities including the bar, restaurant and shopping arcade as well as being able to access beautiful Morningstar Beach where snorkel gear, kayaks, windsurfers and beach equipment are available for rent.

NORTHSIDE

THE NORTHSIDE

By virtue of its northerly orientation, the Northside of St. Thomas, commonly referred to as "Nordside," receives the most rainfall and is consequently the most fertile section of the island.

Magnificent mango, guavaberry, and other mature fruit trees abound along roadways, within valleys and on the steeply sloping hillsides.

In addition to its lush tropical landscapes, panoramic vistas, and relaxed tranquility, the Northside is also the home of several of St. Thomas' most popular tourist attractions such as Magens Bay, Drakes Seat, Mountaintop, St. Peter Greathouse and Mahogany Run Golf Course.

MAGENS BAY

According to popular folklore, Sir Francis Drake used Magens Bay as an anchorage for his fleet and the promontory above the bay, known as Drake's seat, served as his lookout for spotting ships to plunder.

In 1947, philanthropist Arthur Fairchild donated a 58.2-acre tract of land adjacent to Magens Bay to the Government of the Virgin Islands.

Both *National Geographic* and *Condé Nast Traveler* magazines have declared Magens Bay to be one of most beautiful beaches in the world. This magnificent beach stretches more than one mile and is by far the most frequented beach in the Virgin Islands. Facilities include: life guards, snack bar, gift shop, beach gear, watercraft and windsurfer rentals, bathrooms, changing rooms and showers.

The land adjacent to the beach has been designated a nature preserve, managed jointly by the Nature Conservancy, the Virgin Islands Government and the Magens Bay Authority.

Besides enjoying your day at the beach, you may also want to visit the Magens Bay Arboretum originally planted by Arthur Fairchild during the 1920s. Another recommended activity is the guided "Tropical Discovery Hike," through the Magens Bay Preserve emphasizing the history and the natural environment of the area.

PETERBORG

The Peterborg Peninsula separates Magens
Bay on the south from the Atlantic Ocean on
the north. The tranquil sandy beaches and
calm multi-hued waters on the southern side
of the peninsula bordering Magens Bay
contrast sharply with the sheer cliffs, and
deep blues of the usually turbulent waters
just off the northern coast.

Each night as the sun sets an unseen orchestra begins its concert. The music can be heard all over the island, but it is particularly evident in less developed areas such as the Northside.

Let us introduce the musicians:

Antillean tree frog - Continuous "churee - churee"

Whistling frog - High-pitched prolonged whistle often followed by a clicking sound

Coqui - "Ko - KEY" followed by a long pause "Ko - KEY"

White Lipped Frog - "queeee - queeeee - queeee"

SURFING

During the winter months, cold fronts and low pressure systems coming from the North Atlantic and the continental United States generate large ocean swells. Upon reaching the north-facing coasts of Caribbean islands, the swells become breaking waves, which, if conditions are right will be suitable for surfing.

Popular surfing spots on St. Thomas include Hull, Caret, Mandahl, Stumpy and Botany Bays.

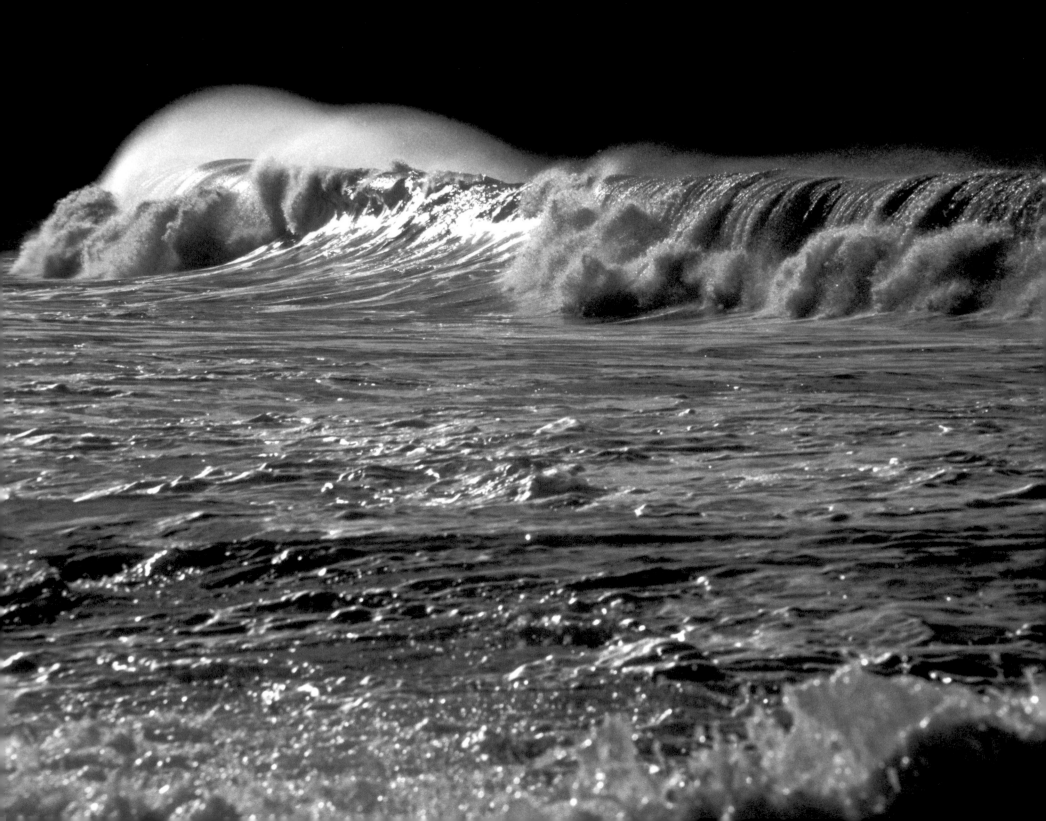

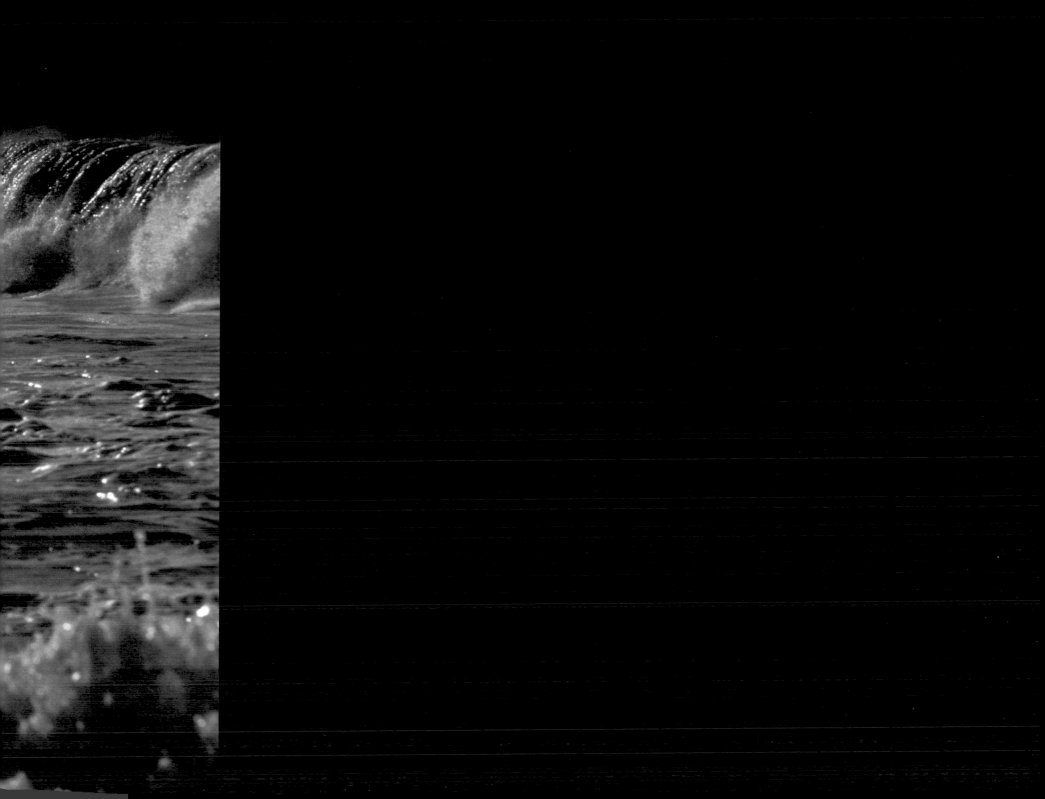

HULL BAY

Hull Bay is primarily frequented by local fishermen who moor their boats in the bay and use the dock, boat ramp and beach to launch their vessels and land their catches. In the winter, surfers take advantage of the north swell to ride breaks with colorful names like "channel," "indigestion" and "danger."

Hull Bay offers a quiet, tranquil beach experience. With its beautiful views, fine snorkeling, local flavor and readily available shade, Hull Bay is an excellent choice for the casual beachgoer.

Additionally, there's a restaurant and bar and a dive shop where you can rent snorkel gear, kayaks and surf boards or arrange for guided kayak, snorkeling or SCUBA diving adventures.

Century Plant

MAHOGANY RUN GOLF COURSE

The Mahogany Run Golf Course opened in 1980.
The course, designed by Tom Fazio, who Golf Digest
describes as "golf's leading designer," is the only golf
course on St. Thomas.

DEVIL'S TRIANGLE

The challenging 13th, 14th, and 15th holes are known as the Devil's Triangle. Make these holes without a penalty stroke and you will be presented with a special "I Survived The Devil's Triangle" certificate from the Pro Shop.

Mountain Top

At 1,542 feet above sea level, the summit of St. Peter Mountain is the highest point on
St. Thomas. Mountain Top, also known as Signal Hill, was used in the 1940s
by the US government as a strategic communications location. It is now one of the most
visited tourist destinations on St. Thomas. The view from the overlook encompasses
most of the islands and cays of the Virgin Islands archipelago, as well as giving a bird's
eye view of the pristine bays of St. Thomas' north shore.

In addition to the view, you can enjoy a famous "Mountain Top Banana Daiquiri,"
created by the illustrious British restaurateur, Conrad Graves, in 1949. You can also
shop at the duty free boutiques and dine at the Mountain Top Grill.

St. Peter Great House and Botanical Gardens

Originally part of the 19th century St. Peter Estate, the newly renovated Greathouse has become a major St. Thomas tourist attraction.

From the expansive observation deck 1,000 feet in elevation, visitors can enjoy a superb vista of the north coast of St. Thomas and the offshore islands and cays extending to St. John and the British Virgin Islands.

The St. Peter Great House also offers fine dining, a gift shop, a botanical garden and a nature trail with waterfalls, fishponds and an aviary.

NELTJEBERG

Neltjeberg Bay, accessible by a rugged dirt road or a trail from Dorothea Bay, is a pristine half-mile sandy beach offering seclusion, good snorkeling on calm days and surfing when the winter ground swells roll in from the north. Just inland from the beach lie the ruins of the 18th century Estate Neltjeberg Sugar Plantation.

VILLAS

In addition to hotels, condominiums and guest houses, St. Thomas
offers a large selection of private villas available for short term rental.

East End

EAST END

Lying in the path of the tradewinds, St. Thomas's East End is the driest part of the island, evidenced by its cactus scrub natural environment.

The East End is blessed with the finest beaches on St. Thomas and has become the activities center of the island, with an assortment of hotels, condominium complexes, restaurants, marinas, dive shops and water sports operations. It is also the gateway to St. John and the British Virgin Islands, with ferries and car barges sailing regularly between the islands.

The two small towns, Red Hook and Smith Bay, provide ample shopping and services for both residents and tourists.

Red Hook

Although somewhat exposed to the easterly tradewinds, the deeply indented harbor at Red Hook offers sufficient protection for most marine related activities, including the ferry and barge port and the modern American Yacht Harbor complex.

SPORT FISHING

Sport fishing in the Virgin Islands can be broken down into three major categories: shoreline fishing, inshore fishing and offshore blue water fishing.

The first category, shoreline fishing, includes fishing from beaches, docks and rocky outcroppings as well as lagoons and shallow water flats. You can fish in the traditional native manner using hand lines or with a rod and reel. Bonefish, jacks, snappers, small sharks, tarpon and barracudas can be caught in the shallow flats and lagoons. You can fish for snapper and other reef fish from the rocks or cast out from the beach for jacks, blue runners, Spanish mackerel and permit.

The second category, inshore fishing, includes bottom fishing and trolling. Using rod and reel or hand line, bottom fishing off of the coral reefs can bring in snapper, parrotfish, rock hind, grunts and blue tang. Spanish mackerel, kingfish, barracudas and amberjacks can be caught trolling around reefs, rocky cays and jutting headlands.

Blue water offshore fishing generally takes place along the north or south drops where water depth descends sharply from about 80 to 120 feet to 600 to 1800 feet. This is where the serious sport fisherman can try their hand against the famed blue marlin, sailfish, tuna, wahoo, bonito and dolphin (mahi-mahi).

SAILING

The Virgin Islands provide just about ideal conditions for sailing in vessels ranging from windsurfers to luxury sailing yachts.

The islands lie in the path of normally moderate and constant tradewinds, truly a sailor's delight. There is a beautiful archipelago of nearby islands and cays to explore and a seemingly endless selection of deep water bays for protected overnight anchorages. In addition to all this, the Virgin Islands offer delightful crystal-clear waters and colorful coral reefs for swimmers, beachgoers, divers and water sports enthusiasts to enjoy.

ROLEX CUP REGATTA

Sailing aficionados often refer to the International Rolex Cup Regatta as the Crown Jewel of the Caribbean. The regatta, hosted by the St. Thomas Yacht Club, first took place in 1974.

The Rolex, as it is called for short, has become a weekend gala with Rolex watches presented to the winners of the various competitions. On shore there are beach parties with live music, drinking and dancing and an Easter Egg hunt for the children.

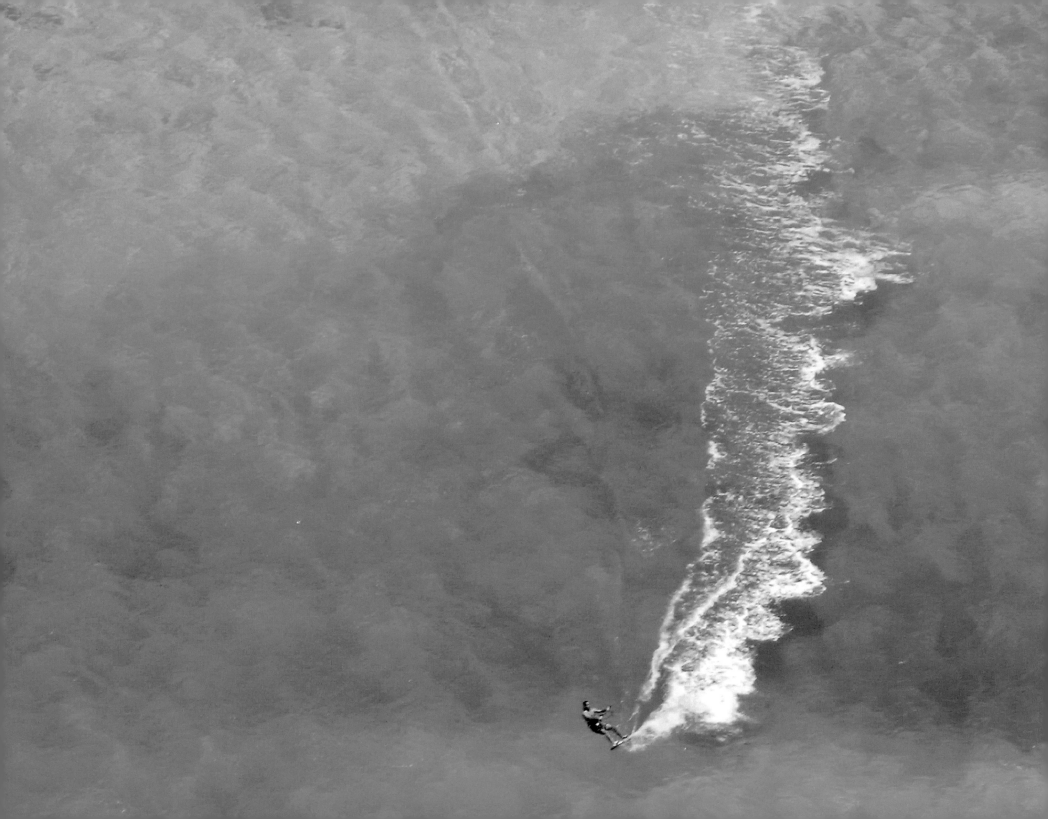

Sapphire Beach

White sand, coconut palms, seagrapes and a magnificent vista of islands and cays all the way to St. John and the British Virgins combine to make Sapphire Beach one of the most beautiful beaches on an island of beautiful beaches.

Sapphire offers great snorkeling over both coral reefs and sea grass beds. There are convenient facilities such as bars, restaurants, gift shops, bathrooms, showers and a beachside dive shop where you can rent beach chairs, snorkel gear and kayaks.

At the nearby Sapphire Beach Marina, you can arrange for just about any kind of water-related activity, including day sails, boat charters, fishing, snorkeling and SCUBA diving expeditions, parasailing, windsurfing and jet ski rentals.

SEAGRAPES

The seagrape is commonly found on St. Thomas'
sheltered beaches, growing at the edge of the sand.
The female tree grows grape-like clusters of fruit,
which turn purple when they are ripe and can be
eaten plain or made into preserves. You can also write
on the leaves with a sharp stick or pointed object, a
characteristic that led them to be used as playing
cards by early setters to the islands.

149

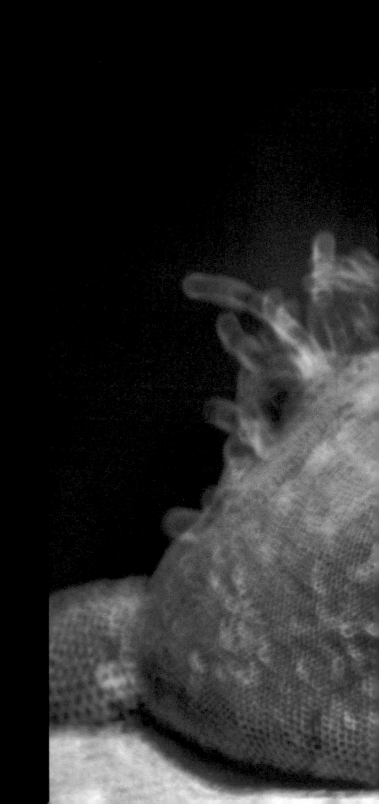

Iguana

LINQVIST BEACH

Linqvist is one of the few easily accessible beaches on St. Thomas that is still free from development. Once the subject of a beach access controversy, Linqvist is now owned by the Virgin Island Government. This fabulous white sand beach offers cooling onshore breezes, magnificent views and shade provided by the seaside vegetation.

Terry White, has been selling her handmade dolls at this same
location at Coki Point for more than 30 years

CORAL WORLD MARINE PARK

The white structure at the end of the headland is Coral World
Marine Park's Undersea Observatory, which extends 100 feet
out into the sea and lies in a depth of about 15 feet. A natural
coral reef surrounds the observatory. At the bottom level of the
air-conditioned facility are large viewing windows where visitors can look out onto the reef.

In addition to this unique attraction, Coral World also features
exhibits such as a 360-degree circular tank housing sharks,
barracudas and other marine predators; an 80,000-gallon salt
water aquarium, a shark pool, a turtle pool, a stingray pool, a
lorikeet garden, a nature trail, two gift shops and two cafés.

COKI POINT

The beach seen in the photo is Coki Point. Funky and fun, Coki
offers soft coral sand, fantastic views and great snorkeling. You
will also find, food stands, bars, hair braiders, a variety of
venders and kiosks where you can rent snorkel gear and beach
accouterments.

Green Turtle & Turtle Hatchling

SMITH BAY

Vendors at roadside kiosks offer fresh fruits and vegetables and local
fisherman sell fresh fish sold from the back of pickup trucks.

The Bananaquit is the official bird of the Virgin Islands.

The Ritz-Carlton

Secret Harbor

JERSEY BAY MANGROVE LAGOON

In the 1960s the extensive Jersey Bay Mangrove Lagoon was the proposed site for a new airport with runways long enough to service intercontinental jet traffic. Fortunately, the project was abandoned and this crucial natural environment has become a Marine Reserve and Wildlife Sanctuary.

Mangrove lagoons protect outlying coral reef communities by filtering out harmful sediments during periods of heavy rain and in the process provide nutrient rich and safe environments for juvenile reef fish, lobsters and other sea creatures. The mangroves also serve as a habitat for birds, animals and wetland plants.

For those interested in mangrove ecology, Virgin Island Ecotours offers guided kayak, snorkeling and hiking tours within the inner mangrove lagoon marine preserve.

169

WEST OF TOWN

Charlotte Amalie Enters the Modern Age

The town of Charlotte Amalie developed around its excellent harbor. By the middle of the 20th Century there was a demand for more services and infrastructure, such as a modern container port, a power plant, an airport, a university, water desalination and sewage treatment systems and cultural and sports centers. These facilities, by and large, were built on the flatlands between the sea and the mountains to the west of town.

Cyril E. King Airport

What is now the modern Cyril E. King Airport was originally a simple runway and airplane hanger built for the use of the US Air Force. In 1950, this facility was upgraded and became the Harry S. Truman Airport. When jet aircraft began flights to the Virgin Islands, the short runway (4,658 feet) could barely accommodate them. Jets could land at the airport, although with some difficulty, but the runway was not long enough to allow them to take off with a full fuel tank. For this reason, jets would have to take off from St. Thomas with only small amounts of fuel and then make a stop at St. Croix to refuel.

In 1976, American Airlines Flight 625, ran off the runway killing 37 of the 88 passengers and crew on board. Although it was pilot error and not the short runway that was ultimately found to be the cause of the crash, American Airlines suspended jet service to St. Thomas after the incident.

Subsequently, the runway was lengthened by cutting away the mountain on one end and filling in the bay on the other. The terminal was renovated and on October 3, 1984, the present airport was dedicated and renamed the Cyril E. King Airport, after a former governor of the Virgin Islands.

The 7,000-foot runway, the same length as the runway at New York's LaGuardia Airport, can now accommodate wide-body jets.

The Pelican

A wonderful bird is a pelican,
His bill will hold more than his belican.
He can take in his beak
Food enough for a week;
But I'm damned if I can see how the helican.

- Often attributed to Ogden Nash but actually
from *The Pelican* by Dixon Lanier Merrith.

Reichhold Center

The Reichhold Center for the Arts was founded by the late Henry H. Reichhold, who came to the Virgin Islands in 1950 and purchased Bluebeard's Castle. His generous contribution of $3,500,000 led to the construction of the Reichhold Center for the Arts in 1976. The Reichhold Center has hosted performances of such notables as Ray Charles, the Moscow Ballet, Count Basie, Roberta Flack, Sarah Vaughan, Nancy Wilson and Itzhak Perlman.

PARADISE JAM

The Paradise Jam, hosted by the University
of the Virgin Islands, is an invitational NCAA
Division I Basketball tournament, drawing the
best men's and women's college teams from
throughout the USA. The games are held at the
university's Sports and Fitness Center during
the November Thanksgiving recess.

BREWERS BAY

Brewers Bay, located just west of the airport, is a popular venue for students from the nearby University of the Virgin Islands and for locals who often host family beach parties there. On weekends local food and drinks are available from roadside vendors.

This coral sand beach, lined with coconut palms and seagrape trees, is said to offer some of the best shelling on the island, especially following storms.

LINDBERGH BAY

The sandy, horseshoe-shaped beach at Lindbergh Bay is lined with coconut palms and seagrapes. Two hotels with bars and restaurants adjoin the beach. A children's playground is located on the west end of the beach.

Previously named Mosquito Bay, Lindbergh Bay got its name in honor of aviator Charles Lindbergh, who landed his plane, "Spirit of St. Louis" on a field just inland from the beach in 1928. This was the same aircraft that Lindbergh piloted the year before when he became the first man to fly solo across the Atlantic Ocean.

WEST END

Secluded Bays

St. Thomas' West End is the least developed section of the island. The bays and beaches of the West End tend to be difficult to access both by land and by sea, keeping them in an almost pristine condition, at least for now.

PLANTATION AGRICULTURE

When the Danish West India Company set out to colonize St. Thomas, their primary motivation was to participate more fully in West Indian trade. St. Thomas was chosen for its excellent harbor and its proximity to both Spanish and British colonies.

Right from the beginning of the colony, however, settlers began to engage in the planting of sugar, tobacco, cotton, indigo and other tropical products; commodities that were so highly valued in Europe at the time. Colonists, using the labor of enslaved Africans, cleared and terraced the rugged mountainous terrain and began to set up plantations on the island. It was the allure of accumulating great wealth in the production of tropical agriculture that later led Denmark to expand its colonial empire to include St. John and St. Croix.

By the mid 18th century the economy that developed around the St. Thomas Harbor had so greatly surpassed the plantation economy that most successful planters left their estates and set up shop as traders and merchants in Charlotte Amalie. They generally kept their plantations, which were left in the hands of overseers, not so much for profit, but for the social status and tax advantages that the country estates provided.

The number of plantations on St. Thomas peaked at 177 in 1725 and then began a steady decline. By the mid 1800s, agriculture had ceased to be an important industry on St. Thomas. Causes for the decline of plantation agriculture, not only on St. Thomas but also for St. John and St. Croix included, a decline in worldwide prices, the depletion of the soil due to poor agricultural practices and natural causes such as hurricanes and droughts.

Botany Bay Plantation Ruins

Bordeaux Bay

"WE GROW FOOD"

The Bordeaux Valley is the site of the Virgin Island Government agricultural project, "We Grow Food."

A large tract of land was divided into about 50 plots ranging from one to five acres each and allocated to local farmers.

The tendency is to have a diversity of agricultural endeavors. In addition to fruits and vegetables, farmers raise ornamentals such as local orchids, some tend bees for honey production and others raise livestock such as goats, sheep, cows and poultry.

Stumpy Bay

Hendrik Bay

Botany Bay

Botany Bay Sunset

Nearby Islands
& Cays

This page: A double rainbow over Hans Lollick

Facing page: A couple is dropped off on Hans Lollick with only a picnic basket, beach blanket and bottle of champagne. The helicopter will return for them later in the day.

Following page: A couple recites wedding vows on Little Hans Lollick.

This page: Passage between Lovango and Congo Cays.

Facing Page: Grassy, Mingo, Lovango and Congo Cays with St. John and Tortola in the background.

THATCH CAY

Within the Virgin Islands archipelago there are
several islands bearing the name Thatch. In
addition to Thatch Cay shown here, there are
also Great Thatch and Little Thatch Islands in
the British Virgins. The name is said to originate
from the infamous pirate Edward Teach a.k.a.
Thatch, better known as Blackbeard.

Thatch Cay Hillside

Christmas Cove, Great St. James

Buck Island

Inner & Outer Brass Cays

Stevens Cay

Hassel & Water Islands

HASSEL ISLAND

Before 1860, Hassel Island was not an island at all. It was a peninsula connected to Frenchtown by a low-lying spit of land. Its strategic location at the southwest entrance to the Charlotte Amalie Harbor, led both the Danes and the British (during the British occupation of the Danish West Indies in the early 19th century) to construct fortifications to defend the harbor.

In the middle of the century, a steam powered marine railway began operation on the peninsula and in 1860, the Danish Government had the connecting isthmus excavated and dredged creating a channel between Charlotte Amalie Harbor and Crown Bay, changing Hassel from a peninsula to an island. The newly-created channel was dubbed Haulover Cut because fishermen used to haul their small vessels over the isthmus rather then have to row or sail around the peninsula.

In the 1930s and 40s, the Paiewonsky family acquired most of the island from the Department of the Interior.

In 1977, the Paiewonskys gave Fort Willoughby, (shown on these pages) to the people of the Virgin Islands and later sold their other holdings on Hassel Island to the National Park.

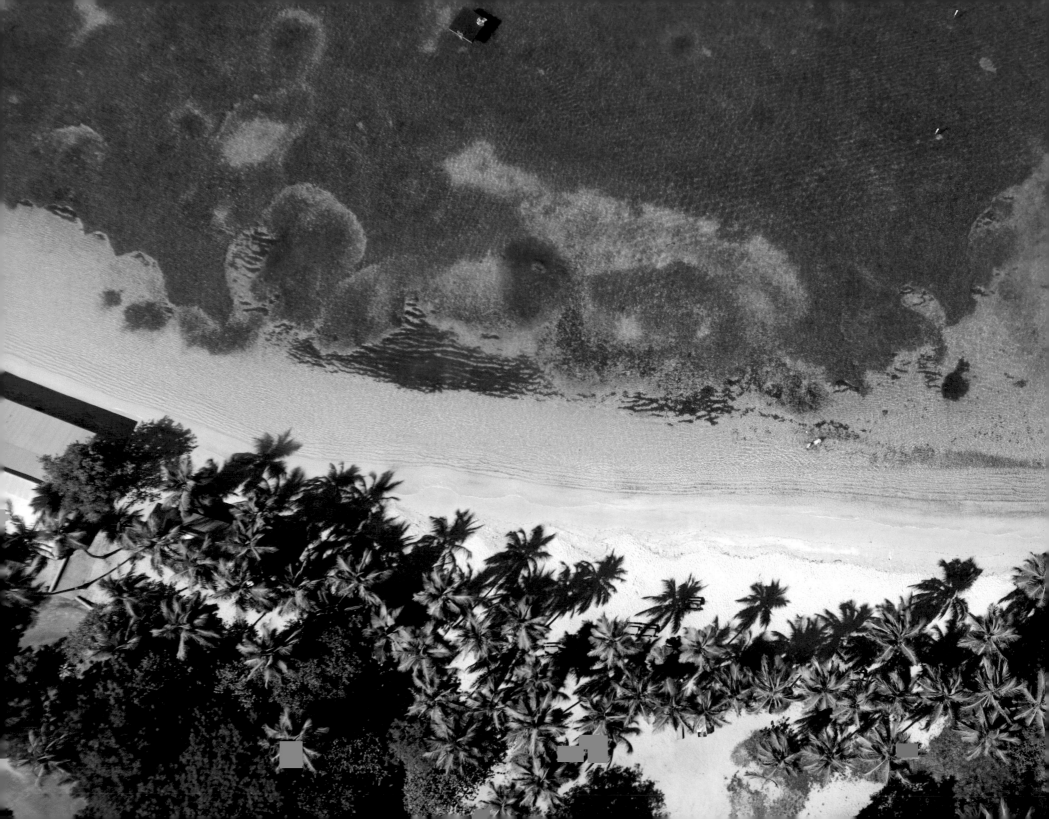

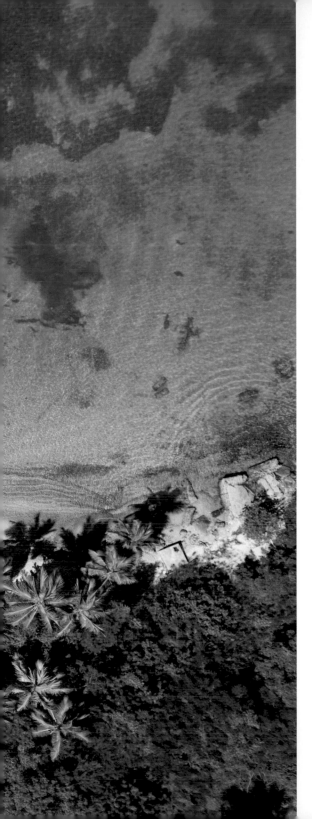

Water Island

Water Island was first inhabited by Amerindian farmers, fishermen and gatherers who migrated from the South American mainland, traveling north through the Leeward Island chain.

In the 16th century, Water Island was frequented by pirates, fishermen, woodcutters and explorers seeking the fresh water that happened to be available on the island, hence the name "Water Island."

In the 18th century, much of Water Island was purchased by free blacks, who managed cotton plantations and raised livestock.

In 1944, the island was acquired by the government of the United States. The purchase was motivated by the island's strategic position overlooking the Submarine Base at Crown Bay. Water Island was turned over to the Department of Defense. The Chemical Warfare Division of the US Army used the island to conduct tests of chemical warfare agents such as Agent Orange until 1950, when the island was turned over to the Department of the Interior.

Acquired by private developers, Water Island is now primarily residential, and has been the fourth official Virgin Island since 1996.

Facing page: Honeymoon Bay on Water Island
Following page: Water Island Aerial

IT'S A GREAT GIG!

Imagine a job where your favorite hobby becomes your life's work.

Through a combination of talent, luck and a thirst for adventure our photographer, Don Hebert, found just that.

Don developed a love of traveling early in life and had journeyed extensively whenever the opportunity presented itself. He always traveled with his camera, and always returned with exceptional photographs. He attended Michigan State and obtained a degree in accounting. After graduation, he left for Europe where he wandered about always with camera in hand.

After six months of the nomadic life, there was no more money and Don reluctantly returned to the States where he began working as an accountant. The job paid well enough, but he found that for him it lacked a sense of satisfaction and personal fulfillment.

After spending a year as an accountant, Don received a call from an old friend informing him of a teaching position that needed to be filled immediately at Saints Peter and Paul High School on St. Thomas. Although he had never even been to the Virgin Islands, he accepted the job and left for the Caribbean shortly thereafter.

The pay wasn't as good, but Don loved teaching, which had the added benefit of affording him sufficient spare time to pursue his hobby of photography. It wasn't long before he had put together a collection of spectacular island photographs.

In 1983, a representative of a local magazine called saying that they had heard that Don had some good slides and asked if he would be willing to sell any. Thus began Don Hebert's career as a professional photographer. Word spread quickly through the "coconut telegraph" and soon he was making more money as a part-time photographer than as a full-time teacher In 1986, he left his teaching job and began shooting photographs full time.

"It's a great gig!" says Don, who loves the job, loves the variety of assignments and absolutely loves the fact that he can earn a living doing what he would do anyway just for fun.

Don Hebert has been photographing the Virgin Islands and the Caribbean for almost two decades. Chosen as one of the top ten photographers to shoot in the Caribbean by *Caribbean Travel & Life*, his work has been featured on the covers of more than 100 publications. He has been published in *Islands Magazine*, *Vogue*, *Caribbean Travel and Life*, *Island Home Magazine*, and *Cruising World*. For more information about Don, visit his website at www.donhebert.com.